We Eat Food That's Fresh!
A Picture Book About Tasting New Foods

¡Comemos Comida Fresca!
Un Libro Sobre Probando Comidas Nuevas

Written by
Angela Russ-Ayon

Illustrated by
Cathy June

Produced by
AbridgeClub.com

All rights reserved. No part of this publication may be reproduced in any form or by any means, electronic, mechanical, photocopying, recording, or otherwise, without written permission from the publishers at AbridgeClub.com. Translated into Spanish and English © 2016 Russ Invision.

Todos los derechos reservados. Se prohíbe reproducer esta publicación total o parcialmente de manera electrónica, mecánica, fotográfica, de grabación, o por cualquier, medio sin el consentimiento escrito de la casa publicadora. Traducción en Español y Inglés © 2016 Russ InVision Company - www. AbridgeClub.com.

Author: Angela Russ-Ayon
Illustrator: Cathy June
Translation: Nancy Lopez-Hernandez
Designer: Tami Miller, www.miller.media
Publisher: Russ InVision Co., www.AbridgeClub.com
Long Beach, CA 90808

ISBN: 978-0-9987090-6-2
IngramSpark, Spanish/English Paperback, 2nd Edition

Printed in the U.S.A.
Music produced by Russ InVision Co. (ASCAP)
Music composition: Bill Burchell
Read by: Jisel Soleil Ayon
Vocals: Angela Russ-Ayon and Tim Russ
Text and music © 2008 Russ InVision
Illustration © Cathy June

We eat food that's fresh.

We eat food that's cooked.

Comemos comida fresca,
Comemos comida cocida.

We eat food prepared from a recipe book.

La Sopa de Vegetales
Vegetable Soup

tomato	el tomate
carrot	la zanahoria
potato	la papa
celery	el apio
onion	la cebolla
bay leaf	la hoja de laurel

El Platano Congelado
Frozen Banana

banana	el platano
wooden stick	el palo de madera
chopped nuts	las nueces picadas

Comemos comida preparada, según un libro de cocina.

We eat food that's chopped.

We eat food that's not.

Comemos comida picada.

Comemos comida entera.

PEPPERS, CORN, SQUASH...in a pot of stew.

PIMIENTOS, MAÍZ, CALABACÍN.

...en sopas o cocidos.

We eat food that's hot.
We eat food that's cold.

Comemos comida caliente.
Comemos comida fría.

We eat food that's canned. We eat food that's dried.

Comemos comida enlatada. Comemos comida deshidratada.

We eat food that's squeezed
for the juice that's inside.

Comemos comida que exprimimos
para beber el jugo interior.

You might just want to try something NEW...

Quizás puedes probar algo NUEVO y DIFERENTE...

FIGS, DATES, KIWI, or some HONEYDEW.

HIGOS, DÁTILES, KIWIS, y MELONES para todos.

We eat food that's baked. We eat food that's grilled.
We eat food that's frozen. We eat food that's chilled.

Comemos comida horneada.

Comemos comida a la plancha.

Comida congelada y también refrigerada.

We eat food from plates.
We eat food from bowls.

Comemos de los platos.
Comemos de los tazones.

We eat food that's ripe or a few days old.

Comida que está maduro o con algunos manchones.

It can't be dirty,
has to be just so.
And, we won't take
food from anyone
we don't know.

NO!
¡NO!

No debería oler extraño,
y no debe estar sucio.
Y no aceptamos comida
de extraños. ¡Que susto!

We eat food that's peeled,
food that's cut in sticks.
We eat food that's dipped,
food that's sliced and mixed.

Comemos comida pelada,
o cortada en palillos,
o sumergido en salsa,
o rebanada y mezclada.

We eat food stir-fried.
We eat food that's creamed.

Comemos comida saltead.
Comemos comida cremosa.

We eat food that's boiled.
We eat food that's steamed.

Comemos comida hervida.
Comemos comida al vapor.

We don't drink too much and lose our appetite, since we need that room for the food we like.

No bebemos mucho para no perder el apetito, porque necesitamos ese espacio para los alimentos sanos.

Breakfast, lunch, and dinner,
morning, noon, or night.
Desayuno, almuerzo, y cena,
en la mañana, tarde, o noche,

www.ingramcontent.com/pod-product-compliance
Lightning Source LLC
Chambersburg PA
CBHW041436010526
44118CB00002B/93